REMBRANDT ETCHINGS

LOOKING AT REMBRANDT'S PRINTS

MICHIEL KERSTEN

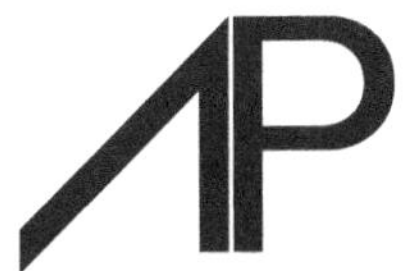

CONTENTS

PREFACE

Rembrandt is justly celebrated as one of the greatest printmakers in European art. His career as a printmaker ran parallel to his career as a painter, but while the paintings are easy to admire, his graphic oeuvre requires a little more from the viewer. For the average museum visitor, prints can at first appear difficult to approach, and the techniques used to create them complicated. This book addresses the need for a clear and concise introduction to Rembrandt's etchings, giving the reader the tools to discover the richness of the prints.

Printmaking techniques are explained in detail and without recourse to jargon. Much attention is given to Rembrandt's contributions to the medium in terms of innovation and experimentation, allowing the reader to fully appreciate their significance.

Historical context adds another dimension to the works of art. A discussion of the function of prints in seventeenth century Europe highlights Rembrandt's unconventional attitude as well as his business sense. Elements of biography give insight into Rembrandt's personal and artistic life, and locate the etchings within the artist's body of works.

A prolific etcher, Rembrandt moved between a range of styles and subjects, including scenes from the Bible, portraits, landscapes, character studies and self-portraits. This book covers each of these genres. By engaging with a number of masterpieces, it sheds light on Rembrandt's genius as a printmaker.

Thorough discussions of prints such as the famous The Hundred Guilder Print and The Three Trees demonstrate Rembrandt's flair for narrative detail, ability to portray emotions and convey moods in black and white. Through the different states the reader can follow Rembrandt's artistic process, and learn how his mastery of the etching technique set him apart.

This book draws attention to the number of ways in which Rembrandt's etchings repay close looking. With a little time and patience, these extraordinary creations reveal their secrets. It soon becomes clear why Rembrandt was better known for his etchings than his paintings in his day.

Liesbeth Heenk

INTRODUCTION

Rembrandt was an exceptional printmaker, and his graphic work has been an unfailing source of inspiration for generations of artists and art lovers. In the marketplace, private collectors and museums have eagerly pursued and collected his prints throughout the centuries.

Even during the artist's lifetime, prints by Rembrandt were copied and forged. Since the beginning of the twentieth century, exhibitions of his etchings have drawn large crowds to museums. Early and rare impressions of his prints have been sold at auctions all over the world, sometimes fetching several hundred thousands of dollars.

Though it is difficult to imagine today, Rembrandt was once probably better known for his etchings than his paintings. This was related to the function of prints before the advent of photography.

What makes Rembrandt's graphic work so special and innovative? How did he make his etchings and what made them different from the prints of his Dutch contemporaries? Who bought the works? And what are etchings anyway?

Rembrandt's prints are in some ways similar to 'slow food'. Looking at Rembrandts requires the undivided time and attention of the beholder, but the rewards make it well worth the effort. This book helps you to look and unravel the secrets of his prints. It's an exciting quest with many surprises. I invite you to come along.

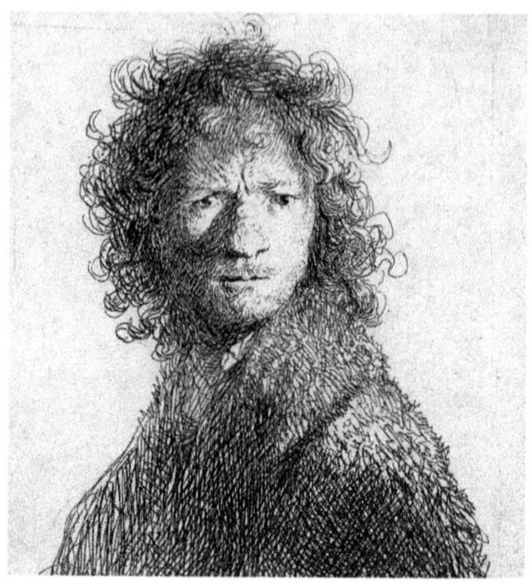

Rembrandt, Self-Portrait frowning, circa 1630, etching, 72 x 60 mm, B. 10.

PRINTMAKING AS A MARKETING TOOL

Today, Rembrandt Harmensz. van Rijn (Leiden 1606-Amsterdam 1669) is especially admired for his paintings. When you think of Rembrandt, you imagine the world-famous Night Watch, the tender embrace in the Jewish Bride, the stern syndics of the Amsterdam cloth-guild and the numerous and enigmatic self-portraits.

In 1628, Rembrandt was discovered by Constantijn Huygens, the highly educated secretary of the Stadholder Frederik Hendrik. This influential art connoisseur considered Rembrandt a promising talent, and praised the young artist for his qualities as a storyteller. In the eyes of Huygens, Rembrandt surpassed even the ancients - higher praise could not be imagined.

Around 1631 Rembrandt, by then a well-known and successful artist, moved to Amsterdam. There he received numerous and prestigious commissions for group portraits, like that of the officers of the militia company of harquebusiers (musketeers or calivermen) under the command of Frans Banninck Cocq, painted for the spacious interior of the newly built wing of the 'Kloveniersdoelen', the guild's main hall. This was the celebrated painting that later became known as the Night Watch. His private clients belonged to the Amsterdam elite.

When Rembrandt married Saskia Uylenburgh from the Frisian upper classes in 1634, he had the world at his feet: he was young, famous and prosperous. Commissions for portraits followed in rapid succession.

In the 1630s and early 1640s Rembrandt was by far the most esteemed portrait painter in the Netherlands. Few artists could charge as much for a portrait. In the first half of the 1650s his standing as an artist remained unchanged, as is shown by the invitation from the burgomasters of Amsterdam to participate in the decoration of the new town hall built in the Dam square (now the Royal Palace).

In the Dutch Golden Age (the seventeenth century), few of Rembrandt's paintings were displayed in public spaces. Unlike the altarpieces by Peter Paul Rubens in the churches of Antwerp, most of Rembrandt's portraits hung behind the closed doors of the fashionable houses of the elite along the canals of Amsterdam.

Some group portraits could be seen in the buildings where civic militias (stadsdoelen) assembled or in guildhalls, such as the Staalhof in Staalstraat, where the syndics of the cloth-guild assessed the quality of materials.

Rembrandt's paintings only came properly out in the open during auctions, where they could be admired by a larger group of people. Still, most contemporaries of Rembrandt probably never saw any of his paintings. The fame of an artist spread by word-of-mouth, the main channel of communication.

There was one other way in which an artist could build up his reputation: by producing and disseminating reproductions of his paintings.

At a time before photography, this was achieved through prints. The famous Flemish artist Peter Paul Rubens employed a group of engravers, and publishers gathered around him to produce printed reproductions of his painted compositions. The resulting black-and-white prints were traded all over Europe. With each print sold, the name and fame of Rubens spread, making his works more costly and sought after.

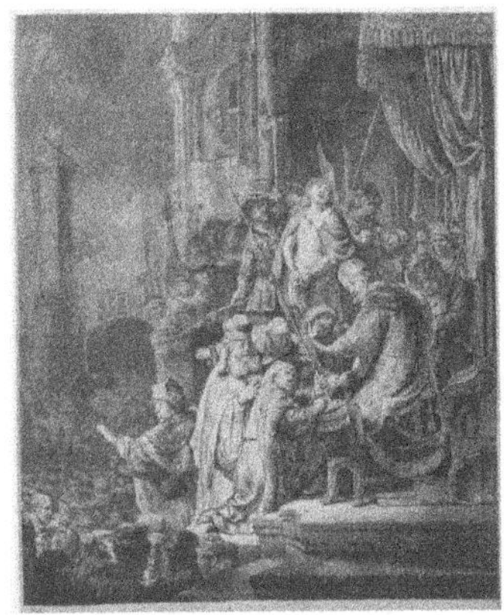

Jan van Vliet, Christ Before Pilate, 1636, etching and engraving, 549 x 447 mm, B 81.

Perhaps Rembrandt was toying with a similar idea when he and Jan van Vliet, his pupil and follower, copied the painting Christ before Pilate in 1636. However, for unknown reasons, the print remained the single experiment of this kind.

Yet, Rembrandt would become one of the most influential and popular printmakers of all time. He did not use prints to reproduce his paintings, but saw them as an independent artistic medium. His etchings of biblical subjects, landscapes, scenes from everyday life and portraits gained widespread fame. At the same time, his prints constituted a solid and regular source of income. A contemporary of Rembrandt may have thought of the artist primarily as a printmaker, not a painter.

AMSTERDAM, A CENTRE OF THE BOOK AND PRINT TRADE

Rembrandt was a brilliant draughtsman. Etching gave him ample opportunity to apply his skills, though on copper plate rather than paper. When finished, the drawing on copper could be printed dozens, if not hundreds, of times. The prints could then be sold by the artist himself, or by booksellers, art dealers and publishers. Rembrandt undoubtedly had his own network of collectors - only a few of his prints were published and sold by others.

In the seventeenth century, Amsterdam was a hub for printers, publishers and book dealers. Some of these had acquired international fame. Most prominent was the Blaeu family, publishers of illustrated and, more importantly, detailed and reliable maps and atlases. The Atlas Novem of 1635 was their most admired work, and the pinnacle of seventeenth century cartography (later published as the Atlas Maior, 1662).

It is known that important print dealers, such as Clement de Jonghe, kept a stock of tens of thousands of prints in their shops. As a consequence the paper trade flourished, especially with France. Some paper mills in the Limousine and the Auvergne were even owned by Dutch paper merchants.

Watermarks are a rich source of information, since one can deduce whether a work may have been printed by Rembrandt himself rather than by later hands with their help.

The book dealers and printers in Amsterdam had extensive international networks, and trade was well organised. Hence, books and prints spread quickly across Europe. The annual book fair in Frankfurt was already an important event for the international book and print trade, and a rich source of business contacts.

An artist who etched and had access to a network of collectors could secure a significant additional income for himself. "If you can print your own prints, then you can print your own money", is a Dutch saying that was already current in the seventeenth century. Rembrandt was aware of this, and proved to be a clever businessman.

Although there were no limited editions, as in later centuries, a rare print was worth much more than one that had been produced in large quantities. Beautiful and rare prints made collectors empty their money-bags.

Prints on valuable paper, such as Chinese or Japanese varieties, vellum or even silk, were eagerly sought after by collectors. Rembrandt used some 350 different kinds of paper. At times, he printed on rough, hard or tinted paper. Other times he used soft, fine grain white paper, or even extremely thin and smooth Japanese or Chinese paper.

The choice often depended on the subject of the print, but even more on the graphic effects that he wanted to achieve. At times, Rembrandt even tinted the paper with watercolour or ink to evoke a certain mood, or to enhance the atmosphere in the image.

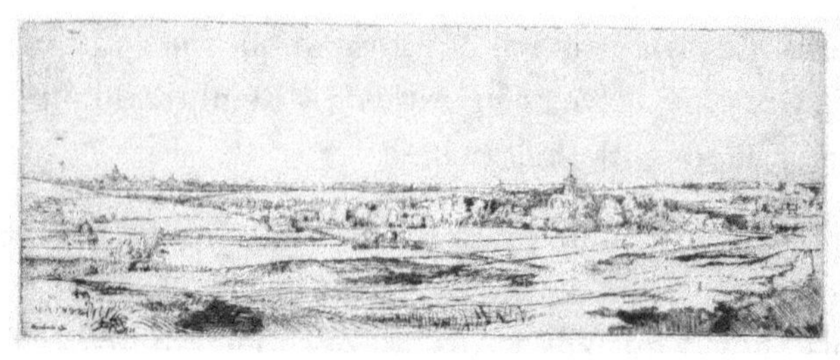

Rembrandt, View of Bloemendaal and Haarlem, etching and drypoint, 120x 319 mm, B. 234.

EXPERIMENTS IN BLACK AND WHITE

Throughout his career, Rembrandt experimented profusely with ways of printing his etchings by applying more or less ink to the plate. Sometimes he would even leave an extremely thin layer of ink on the plate, referred to as plate tone, which can radically change the atmosphere of an image.

Like no other, Rembrandt used different graphic techniques within a single print to achieve certain effects. He combined etching with drypoint, and enhanced the blackness of certain lines with an engraving tool called burin. He was adventurous, especially towards the end of his career.

Without exaggerating too much, one can say that no prints by Rembrandt are identical, provided that they were printed by the master himself. A book about Rembrandt the etcher is for that reason also a book about graphic experimentation.

Understanding the various techniques is a necessity if one wants to fully appreciate Rembrandt's prints. Therefore, the graphic techniques used by Rembrandt will be explained in more detail below.

GRAPHIC ARTS: ENGRAVING AND ETCHING

Rembrandt used three printmaking techniques: engraving, etching and drypoint. All three are intaglio processes, which means that the image is printed from ink-filled lines or textures scratched or etched into a metal plate.

Intaglio printing is the opposite of relief printing. In relief printing, of which woodcuts and books are examples, the inked portions of the block rise above the blank areas.

The areas of a surface that were not to be printed were cut away by a woodcutter, or, for books, the letter cutter.

Relief printing is the oldest of the graphic processes: the first block books appeared just before 1400. The earliest intaglio prints date from around 1450.

Engraving is the oldest intaglio technique, and uses a copper plate as a base. It was developed by gold- and silversmiths to embellish weapons, jewelry and other precious metal objects.

An engraving is made by cutting a line with a burin, a kind of chisel with a sharp triangular point, into a flat, finely polished, copper plate. Engraving is painstaking work, demanding the utmost of the craftsmanship of the artist. The engraver must proceed carefully, since cutting deeper into the copper plate produces wider and deeper grooves, eventually printing darker and wider lines.

When engraving, the artist can only push his burin forward, cutting a groove into the plate.

Characteristically, an engraved line starts with a sharp point and gradually swells as the engraver pushes his burin deeper into the copper. Towards the end, the line diminishes in width and ends in a point as the tip of the burin reaches the surface.

In order to obtain a curved line, the plate, rather than the hand holding the burin, is turned. While the artist pushes the burin forward with one hand, the other hand rotates the plate, thus engraving a curved line. To be able to turn the plate, the artist places it on a flat leather cushion.

As a result of this method, engravings always display gradually curving lines, and never jagged grooves with sharp corners. By putting the lines closer together, by applying cross hatching, or by cutting the parallel hatching deeper into the plate, the artist can suggest shadows, tones and create a sense of depth and volume. Engraving requires an enormous amount of practice, and substantially limits the artist's ability to draw freely and spontaneously.

The etching technique was developed to give the artist more artistic freedom. To make an etching, the artist starts with a flat, polished copperplate. This plate is covered with a soft, acid resisting layer most often made from beeswax. Subsequently, the front is blackened with soot by holding a candle under the plate.

With an etching needle, the artist is able to draw as freely as with a pencil or chalk on paper.

By drawing with the etching needle the artist removes the wax layer, exposing the shiny copper plate. As these bright yellow lines contrast with the matte, dark surface of the wax layer, the artist can easily keep track of the progress of his drawing. Mistakes can be corrected by recovering lines with etching ground.

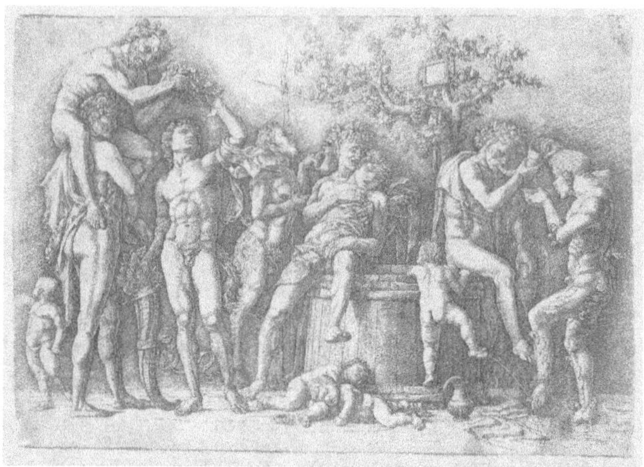

Andrea Mantegna (1430/31–1506), Bacchanal with a Wine Vat, 1470s, 298 x 438 mm. The image is built up with diagonal hatchings.

The proper etching process starts after the artist has finished his design. He then pours an acid, such as hydrochloric acid, over the front of the copper plate. In the places where the drawn lines have removed the acid-resisting wax layer, the acid bites into the exposed copper surface. The more aggressive the acid, the faster and deeper it will bite grooves into the plate. Instead of pouring the fluid, the artist can immerse the plate in an earthenware tray filled with acid.

The longer the plate stays in the acid, the deeper the grooves. Deep grooves hold more ink and will result in deep black lines. Biting the plate is often a matter of trial and error, and relies on the experience of the artist. Once the etching process is complete, the artist has to clean the plate, and remove the rest of the wax layer.

Rembrandt most likely preferred a mildly aggressive acid, giving him more control over the etching process. He sometimes etched his plates several times.

The result of the etching is a copperplate in which the drawing shows itself as grooves in the surface of the plate. The plate is then ready to be printed.

First of all, the plate is warmed slightly to increase the fluidity of the ink, so that it runs smoothly into the grooves.

With the assistance of a tampon made of leather strips, the ink is spread out evenly over the entire surface of the plate. Now the painstaking work of cleaning the whole surface begins, by wiping away the inks with bits of cloth. The last traces of ink are removed from the surface with the ball of the artist's thumb.

This is a difficult task, as the ink needs to be wiped away from the surface, but left untouched in the grooves. Eventually, the surface is shiny and clean and the lines filled with ink.

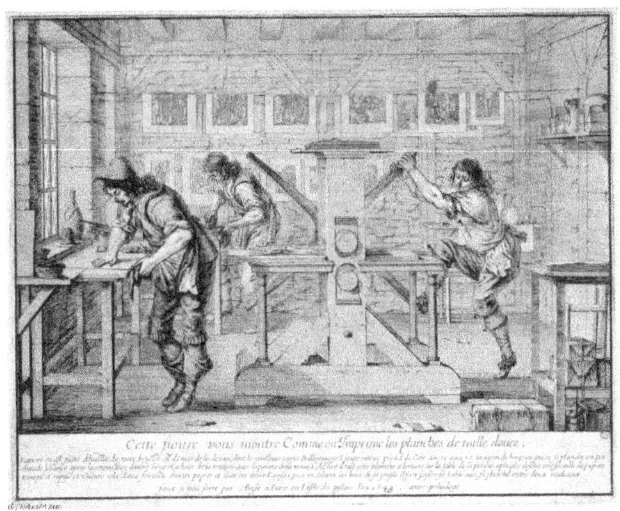

Abraham Bosse (1602–1676), A Printer's Workshop, etching, 261 x 362 mm.

In this print from the handbook on engraving and etching by Abraham Bosse (1645) all the stages of printmaking are shown. In the back of the workshop, a printer smears the ink on the plate with a tampon. To the left, a workshop assistant wipes off the last bits of ink from the plate's surface with the ball of his thumb, at the same time carefully leaving the ink in the grooves of the plate. In the middle, a printer turns the wheel of the press with hands and feet, thus moving the plate, paper and felt lying on a wooden board between two rollers made of oak wood. In front of the window stands a little coal-pan. This has been used to heat the plate to increase the fluidity of the ink. The prints are hung to dry on taut lines.

Finally, the actual printing can start. The copperplate is placed reverse down on the board of an etching press. A sheet of damp paper is put on top and subsequently a piece of felt. The board is then fed through the press. The rollers of the press put immense pressure on the felt, pushing the paper into the ink-filled grooves and around the edges of the plate. The ink sticks to the damp paper, and when the paper is pulled from the plate reveals the mirror image of the engraved design.

As the ink is still wet, the printer hangs the freshly printed paper on a line to dry. The edges of the plate are visible as an indentation in the paper, and can be felt with a fingertip. This is one of the most important characteristics of an etching. A modern reproduction may display an indentation, but one can never feel it.

STATES: STAGES OF THE ARTISTIC PROCESS

When working on an image, an artist may wish to review his progress. This can be done more accurately by printing a test image on a piece of paper rather than observing the etching ground. The technical term for a print of an unfinished design is "a state".

A different state - a new version - comes into being every time the artist makes an alteration to the plate, even if the changes are hardly visible. Rembrandt completed some etchings without trial prints (proofs), but for most of his works several states, often two or three, are known.

As many as eight states of the large print Christ Shown to the People (1655) survive. Different states are interesting since they often showcase the trial and error involved in the artistic process. In addition, they are interesting reflections of the mindset of the artist while creating the image.

Specialised art historians have mapped all the states of Rembrandt's etchings, a complicated task as states sometimes only differ in a few, small lines, perhaps only visible with a magnifying glass.

States are also interesting for another reason, as some alterations to the plates have been made long after the death of Rembrandt.

Naturally, plates altered or restored by other artists are a lot less valuable.

Buying a Rembrandt etching is a complicated matter, and demands extensive knowledge.

Not only of prints and states, but also of paper, another important criterion for judging the authenticity of a Rembrandt print.

In the seventeenth century, paper was expensive. Not even small scraps of paper were discarded, and especially not proof impressions.

Just like nowadays, rare prints were prized by art connoisseurs. It seems that Rembrandt occasionally even produced small runs of a specific state of an etching just to satisfy the demand from collectors. A clever method of earning money, a craft Rembrandt understood very well.

SHOWN HERE ARE two different stages of The three crosses: state I (above) and the completely reworked state IV (below).

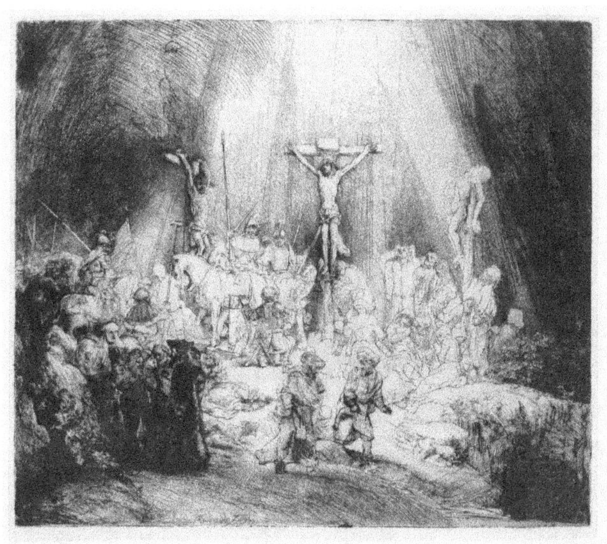

Rembrandt, The three crosses, drypoint and burin, 385 x 450 mm, B 78.

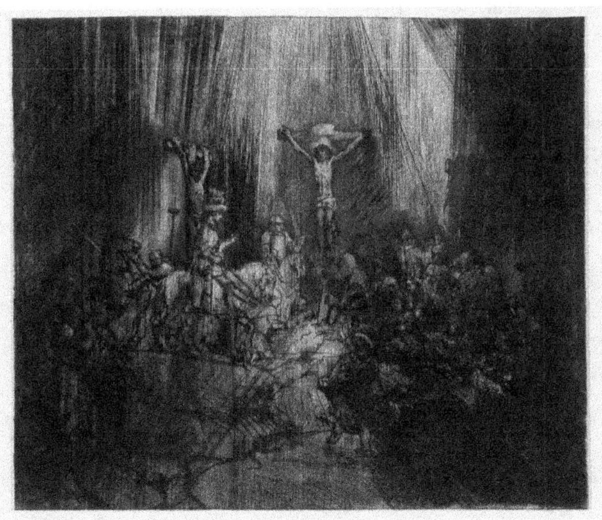

Rembrandt, The three crosses, drypoint and burin, 385 x 450 mm, B 78.

ANOTHER GRAPHIC TECHNIQUE: DRYPOINT ETCHING

Rembrandt also made so-called drypoint prints, sometimes erroneously called etchings in drypoint. Drypoints are made by scratching the lines of the design with a needle directly into the copper plate. Rembrandt used this technique often, and also in combination with etching. Sometimes he would even engrave certain lines with a burin.

Judging from the large number of drypoints in his oeuvre, Rembrandt must have loved the look and feel of a drypoint etching. The most likely explanation is that scratching with the needle into the surface of a plate in a way resembles sketching with a pen and ink. The artist can also control the final results better than with etching - the biting process could sometimes bring about unexpected and unwanted results.

Scratching directly into the plate may easily go wrong. Was a mistake a disaster for the artist? No, but correcting an error was a time-consuming task. The artist sometimes used a burnisher, a metal, spoon-like utensil with a bent, flat top, to polish away a line. To flatten the surface, the back has to be hammered slightly upwards, to compensate for the hollow caused by burnishing. Rembrandt normally worked with thin plates, making hammering and burnishing easier.

Copper has the advantage of being a rather soft metal: scratching lines in a plate with a needle-like instrument requires relatively little force.

Scratching leaves a burr along the line. With its sharp edges, the burr will retain a tiny bit of printing ink, even after the surface of the plate has been wiped. This results in soft-edged lines with a fuzzy quality and velvety hue.

The burr wears away quickly when printing, meaning that an artist can only produce a limited number, perhaps twenty, good impressions of a print made with drypoint. After that, the fuzzy black quality of the lines disappears. A worn drypoint produces grey lines.

A fine print - and this applies to all engravings, etchings and drypoints - is distinguished by sharp-edged, deep, black lines. The finest impressions of drypoint etchings can be printed on very smooth and extremely thin paper from Japan or China.

As this kind of paper is less absorbent, the ink dries slower than on European paper, enhancing the typical velvety character of a drypoint-line better than any other paper.

Early prints of Rembrandt's etchings are now extremely rare, and as a consequence, expensive. However, auction houses and art dealers all over the world still offer original Rembrandt prints. Most of these etchings were printed in the eighteenth and nineteenth centuries from worn plates.

Invariably, these prints are rather dull: the lines are no longer black, and as the surface becomes rougher it cannot be cleaned completely, resulting in a grey print.

For a few hundred dollars, these prints can be bought from various art dealers, auction houses or even eBay.

Prints with black, crisp lines from the seventeenth century, perhaps printed by Rembrandt himself, will fetch ten to twenty times as much at auction, and sometimes even more.

Buying a Rembrandt can be perilous, but even a grey and worn impression of a plate by Rembrandt is and remains an original Rembrandt.

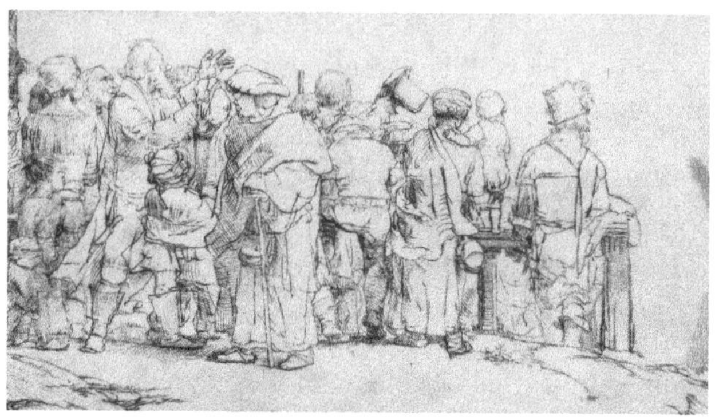

Rembrandt, detail of Christ presented to the people, B 76.

The image shows the typical angular lines of dry point-work and the hazy, fluffy quality of the lines, as a result of the burr along the edges of the lines scratched into the plate by the artist. This burr wears quickly. After some twenty impressions the burr will be worn away resulting in grey lines.

THE PAINTER-ENGRAVER

Many etchers and engravers in the seventeenth century concentrated on reproducing the paintings of other artists. With lines and crosshatching, they attempted to imitate the tones, hues and colors of a painting.

These prints are often made with great skill and craftsmanship, but remain mere copies of paintings. Although such prints could be instrumental in spreading the name and fame of an artist, they dwell at a lower level in the hierarchy of the arts.

Original work was more highly esteemed. In the case of the graphic arts this meant a print designed (invented or deliniavit), etched (fecit), printed and published (excudit) by an artist himself. The Latin terms, stemming from art historical tradition, were often engraved directly on plates, proving the importance of identifying the role of those involved, especially when artists collaborated.

An artist who creates his own compositions and executes these in graphic arts is called a "peintre-graveur" [painter-engraver]. Great painters were often also important and innovative printmakers. From Lucas van Leyden to Picasso, and from Albrecht Dürer to Édouard Manet. These artists did not look down on graphic arts as tools for reproduction, but regarded printmaking as a different, but equally important, side of their artistic work.

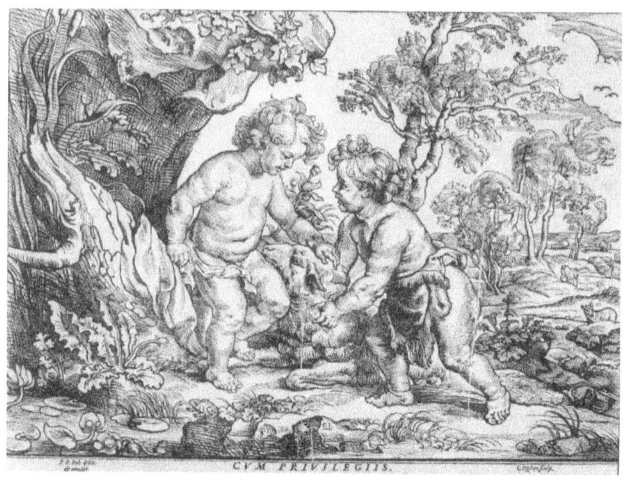

The infants Jesus and Johannes de Doper, print designed and published by Peter Paul Rubens (delin. & exudit), engraved by Christoffel Jegher (sculp.). The cum privilegiis, revers to the privilege given by the authorities to publish this print, a sort of copy right protecting the print.

Prints were artworks in their own right, and could be useful in terms of sales. This also applies to Rembrandt: his enormous production and experimentation demonstrate his commitment to printmaking. He must have enjoyed working on his prints, and valued his etchings highly.

For an artist who produced such groundbreaking work, anything else would be inconceivable.

PRINTMAKING AND COLLECTION AS A SOURCE OF INFORMATION AND INSPIRATION

Not all Netherlandish artists travelled to Italy to see and study the ruins from Roman times, or to admire the works of Michelangelo, Raphael, Titian and Caravaggio, the great artists of the Renaissance and the Baroque.

Still, Northern European artists were generally well aware of the latest developments in the visual arts in Italy, and the archaeological findings of Greek and Roman works. Printmaking played a huge role in the dissemination of knowledge and the artistic innovations of the Italian Renaissance artists.

Prints with reproductions of paintings and sculptures were traded throughout Europe, and provided valuable information for artists. Rembrandt had, like other important artists (e.g. Peter Paul Rubens), a huge collection of art on paper, prints as well as drawings. In his 'kunstcaemer' in his house in Jodenbreestraat in Amsterdam (now the Rembrandt House Museum) he kept a collection of more than 8,000 works on paper in numerous folders.

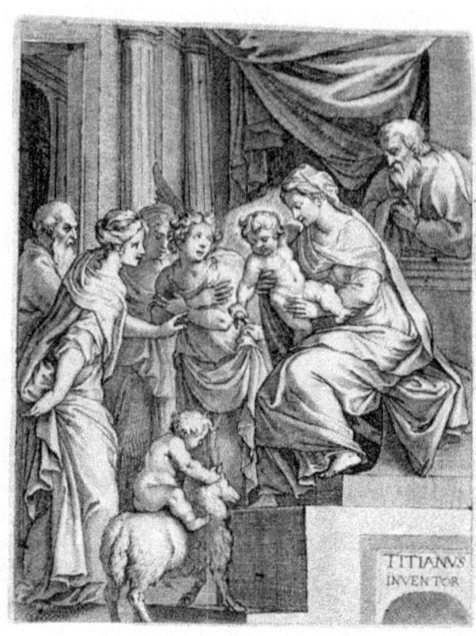

Cornelis Cort (1553-1578) after Titian, The Holy Family with John the Baptist, Saints, and Angels, engraving, 1570.

These artworks were purchased at auctions, from booksellers and from collectors in Amsterdam. Rembrandt spent a fortune on his collection, and it was one of the reasons he went bankrupt in 1656.

ARTISTIC RIVALRY: REMBRANDT AND DÜRER

Prints did not only disseminate knowledge, but could also be a wonderful source of inspiration. Art in the seventeenth century was largely governed by rules and tradition. The complete artistic freedom widely enjoyed today did not exist in those days. The depiction of a particular subject was ruled by convention, and artists studied each other's work thoroughly. Typically, Renaissance and Baroque artists, like Rembrandt, tried to refine the admired works of a predecessor or contemporary artist. In art historical terms, this is known as 'aemulatio', to emulate an admired work of art by another artist - a kind of artistic rivalry.

An informative example of this kind of artistic rivalry is the large Rembrandt etching, The Death of the Virgin from 1639. The subject of this etching is not found in the Bible, but originates from a thirteenth century collection of legends about the saints, known as the Legenda Aurea (The Golden Legend), attributed to Jacob de Voragine.

The story in The Golden Legend recounts how the Twelve Apostles were transferred as by a miracle to the deathbed of the Virgin, just like Christ had promised his mother. The death and ascension of the Virgin were beloved subjects in art from the Middle Ages onwards.

Rembrandt's depiction differs from the story in the Golden Legend: not only are the Twelve Apostles present, but also countless other people, both young and old.

In the apocryphal legend, the Virgin is being handed a palm leaf, a detail that is lacking in Rembrandt's image.

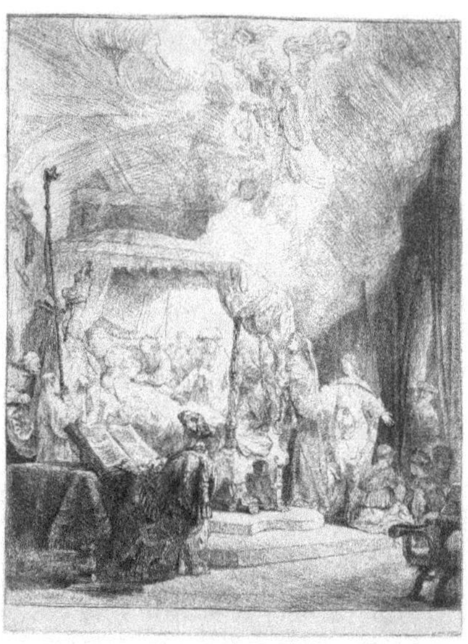

Rembrandt, The Death of the Virgin, 1639, etching and drypoint, 409 x 315 mm, B 99.

A year before Rembrandt begun this etching, he bought a series of woodcuts by Albrecht Dürer depicting the Life of the Virgin at an auction in Amsterdam.

It must have inspired Rembrandt, as he borrowed numerous details in his The Death of the Virgin from Dürer's woodcuts. The boy with the huge staff can be traced back to Dürer's Death of the Virgin (first image below), whereas the angels and clouds can be found in the woodcut of the Birth of the Virgin (second image below).

In the hands of Rembrandt, The Death of the Virgin became a swirling composition. The divine character is represented by a bright stream of light falling from the sky,

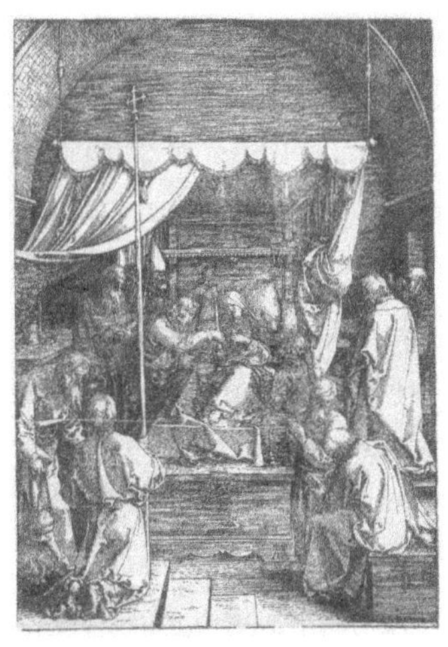

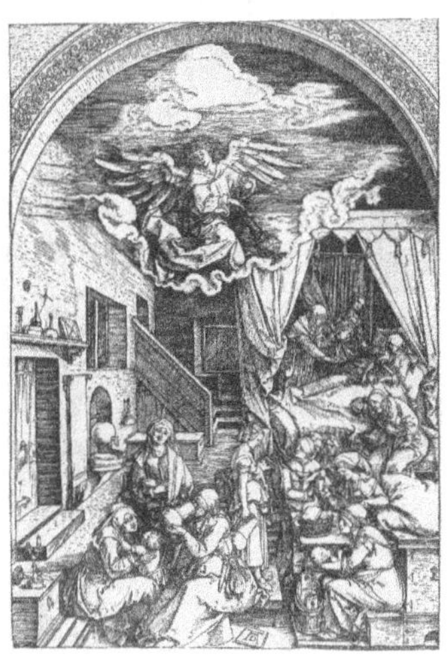

onto the deathbed of Mary. The upper part of this image is made up of a few rather rough and sketchy lines; contrastingly, the foreground with the apostle reading is meticulously worked out.

The main scene with the Virgin and the figures directly behind her bed is carefully drawn yet consists of only a few lines, often no more than contours. Most of the paper remains blank. As a result, the celestial light falls directly onto the main scene. It immediately draws the eye of the beholder to the human and divine drama unfolding around the bed.

The inclusion of countless narrative details is typical of Rembrandt. Next to the Virgin stands an apostle or a doctor of the church, supporting her head by lifting the pillow with his left arm. In his other hand, he clutches a cloth with which he wipes her face. Another figure holds her wrist, checking the pulse.

A man with a mitre, most likely Saint Peter, looks resigned and gloomy. Next to him stands a choirboy with a long staff, a motif, as we have seen above, borrowed from Albrecht Dürer. A similar expression to that of Saint Peter, almost impassive, can be found on the face of the old woman next to the man holding the Virgin's wrist. A younger woman beside her seems more interested in the action around the bed than sad. Other women in the image cry or pray, and their grief can almost be felt by the beholder.

In front of a man with spread arms (probably Saint John the Baptist), a young woman is praying, her face serene. This motif immediately catches our attention, since it is rendered by Rembrandt with only a few lines, convincingly suggesting a beam of light falling directly onto these two figures. The same can be said about the man who has just opened the curtains, and is about to enter the room.

The areas to the right and left are kept quite dark, functioning like the wings of a theatre set, leading the eye of the beholder to the Virgin and the divine transfiguration: the angel guarding Saint Mary who will accompany her soul to heaven.

The contrast between the darker, more elaborate, parts of the composition and brighter areas, sparingly rendered with a few sketchy lines, convincingly draws attention to the main scene - the death of the Virgin. The dark foreground with the velvety lines is distinctive: Rembrandt accentuated this part of the composition by scratching with a needle directly into the copper plate.

As far as we know, this is the first time Rembrandt used drypoint in this way to enhance the contrast between light and dark, his famous chiaroscuro (stark contrast between light and shadow), so typical of his paintings.

REMBRANDT'S MOST FAMOUS ETCHING

Some ten years after The Death of the Virgin Rembrandt completed an etching that is considered the most important print in his oeuvre: The Hundred Guilder Print.

This curious title is based on a story about how Rembrandt bought a copy of his own print at an auction for 100 guilders, a small fortune, and about half the annual income of a craftsman. If this story is true, it illustrates Rembrandt's keen eye for business, buying his own print to create the impression that it was rare and valuable. This is a proven strategy in the art world, and still used today by gallery owners and dealers in contemporary art.

In The Hundred Guilder Print, contrasts between light and dark lead our eye directly to the main scene: Christ in the act of blessing. He stands almost in the centre of the composition, watched by a multitude of onlookers: young and old, rich and poor, healthy and sick. Rembrandt has not depicted a specific passage from the Bible, but brought together several events described in chapter 19 in the Gospel of Matthew in one image.

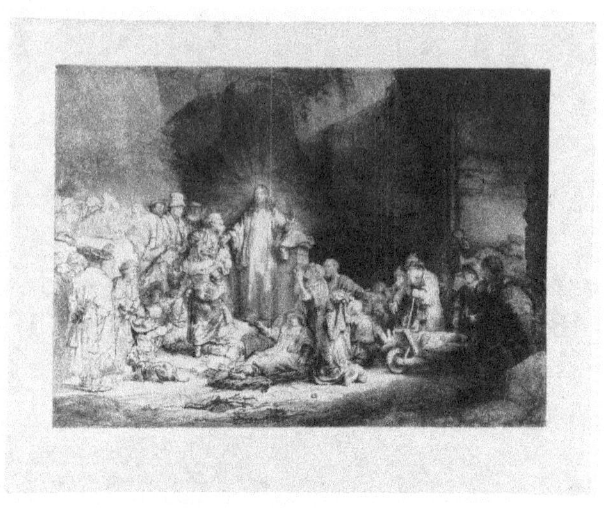

Rembrandt, The Hundred Guilder Print, circa 1639-1649,
etching, drypoint and burin, 278 x 388 mm, B. 74.

A woman with a baby cradled in her arms stands near Christ, who looks at her intently. A boy tugs at his mother's skirt, pointing with his finger towards Christ.

This scene reminds us of Christ's saying "Suffer little children, and forbid them not, to come unto me: for of such is the kingdom of heaven" (Matthew 19:14). These words of rebuke were provoked by the disciples, who tried to prevent a group of mothers with their children from coming close to Christ so as to have their children blessed.

We can see how Saint Peter – with the bald head and beard - tries to hold back the woman with the baby in her arms. He seems transfixed by Christ: all his attention is concentrated on his figure. Christ, however, softly pushes Saint Peter to the side with his right hand.

The Gospel of Matthew further describes how a group of ill and lame people followed Christ, who blessed and cured them. In the image one can see the sick being brought to Christ. "Jesus", writes Matthew, "went about all the cities and villages, teaching in their synagogues, and preaching the gospel of the kingdom, and healing every sickness and every disease" (Matthew 9:35).

The same Gospel describes a series of discussions between Christ and the Sadducees and Pharisees, in which the latter tested Christ. One question was on the topic of marriage and divorce. The Pharisees asked Christ: "Is it lawful for a man to divorce his wife for just any reason?". "...What therefore God has joined together, let no man separate", Christ famously replied. In the upper left corner of the print we can see the Pharisees debating and discussing the new teachings. The self-assured, disdainful smirk on the face of one of the Pharisees says it all: they attach no importance to the words spoken by Christ.

Next to Saint Peter, Rembrandt has meticulously drawn the sitting figure of a richly dressed young man. He looks pensive, as he rests his head against his right hand, pondering Christ's answer to his question about how to gain eternal life. Jesus had answered him: "If you would be perfect, go, sell what you possess and give to the poor, and you will have treasure in heaven". Rembrandt's skillful portrayal of the boy makes it clear that he is facing a very difficult decision regarding whether to leave his wealth behind. Afterwards, Christ said to his disciples: "It is easier for a camel to go through the eye of a needle than for a rich person to enter the kingdom of God." As a visual reminder of the parable, Rembrandt has included a camel in background, to the right.

This image of the preaching Christ with his hand raised in blessing, "Beati pauperes spiritu" (Blessed are the poor in spirit, Matthew 5:3), is unique in the sense that it is the only print in which Rembrandt has combined several different biblical scenes in one image.

LOOKING AT PRINTS TAKES TIME

One has – as always with Rembrandt's prints – to spend some time looking at the images to discover and relish all the wonderful details. Although the central theme of the large print is clear at first glance, the mastery of Rembrandt lies in the countless different facial expressions of the bystanders, the Pharisees and the sick that are brought to Christ. Every face, every figure, every attitude is unique, and conveys a new emotion.

Remarkable is also Rembrandt's habit of drawing one figure with just a few outlines, while others are meticulously crafted with a wealth of detail. Though many figures are essentially silhouettes, the composition as a whole does not make an unfinished or unbalanced impression, as light unifies all compositional elements. The left side of the print consists mostly of quickly outlined figures, with the paper left almost blank, seemingly bathing in light. From an invisible source, a beam of light falls on Christ, and a blind old man who is accompanied by his wife as well as an old woman with a crippled man lying in a wheelbarrow.

If one squints, one can observe the ingenuous way in which Rembrandt has built up the composition. Although it may initially seem like a random gathering of people, Rembrandt's image is carefully composed. All the figures fall roughly within two triangles. The top of one of these triangles runs over the heads of the Pharisees to the right and cuts through the wheelbarrow, with the baseline running under the figures from the left-hand side of the image.

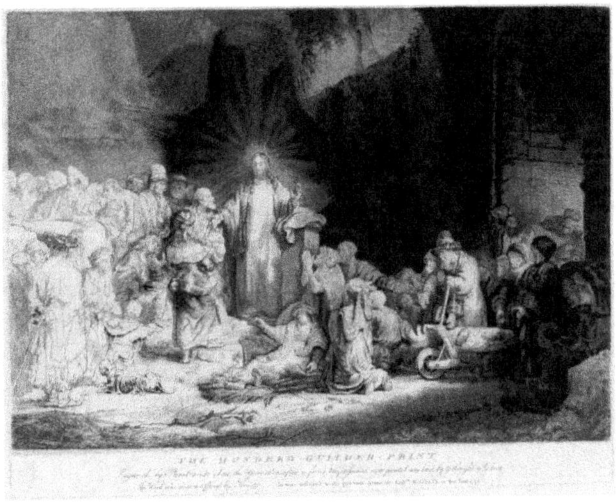

Rembrandt, The Hundred Guilder Print, 'restored' and printed by William Baillie, circa 1775.

On the right side of the image, the figures are also caught within the lines of a triangle. No figure or gesture is redundant, and all components are interconnected. The figural group in the middle of the image smoothly leads our eyes from the woman lying in front of Christ to a woman kneeling in prayer.

Our gaze flows effortlessly from the pointing boy and his mother, to the rich young man and then to the woman with the infant via Saint Peter to Christ. Even within the triangles, smaller figural groups are connected.

Take a look at the figures in the middle foreground - together they form a triangle, of which the top is made up by the man with the outstretched arm. That arm leads the eye back to the hand of the blind man, supported by his wife.

As everything is interconnected, the composition makes a balanced impression, despite the diversity of the figures and attitudes. At first glance, the image seems made up of somewhat haphazard elements, but if you look closely you will see that Rembrandt has thought about every figure, every gesture and every line. Herein lies the secret of his virtuosity.

The Hundred Guilder Print was considered to be the most important etching in Rembrandt's oeuvre in the eighteenth and nineteenth centuries. After the artist's death in 1669, the image became immensely popular and was printed countless times. In the second half of the eighteenth century, the original, but worn, copper plate came into the possession of Captain William Baillie (circa 1724-1810).

He deepened the existing grooves, and then printed 100 copies of this 'restored' version of Rembrandt's plate. Afterwards, Baillie divided the plate into several smaller pieces, which in turn were printed numerous times by the English captain. Could there be a better example of Rembrandt's undiminished popularity in these centuries?

PAINTING IN BLACK AND WHITE

Rembrandt's graphic oeuvre is full of experimental works. Sometimes he would sketch a landscape with just a few lines with an etching needle, as if drawing from nature. Other times, the artist completed thousands of cross and parallel hatchings to imitate the characteristics of a painting.

A painter has a brush and paints at his disposal to create tone. A draughtsman or printmaker has it much harder in this respect: only through hatching or by making lines darker or lighter can he suggest tone, hue, volume, light or shade. In the seventeenth century, artists tried to invent and develop methods of printing tone.

Rembrandt sometimes left a thin film of ink on the surface of the plate. Just as in his experiments with different kinds of paper, he used plate tone to reinforce the atmosphere or mood of an image.

As a painter, Rembrandt loved to accentuate the contrast between light and dark as a means to highlight the protagonists in the composition and their facial expressions. This stark contrast is often described in art literature using the Italian expression 'chiaroscuro'. It was Rembrandt's trademark. No other artist, with the exception of the Italian painter Caravaggio, achieved such dramatic chiaroscuro effects. Rembrandt often chose to depict night scenes, lit by candles, as this gave him ample opportunity to include intense contrasts between light and dark in his compositions. As a printmaker, he used chiaroscuro in his etchings.

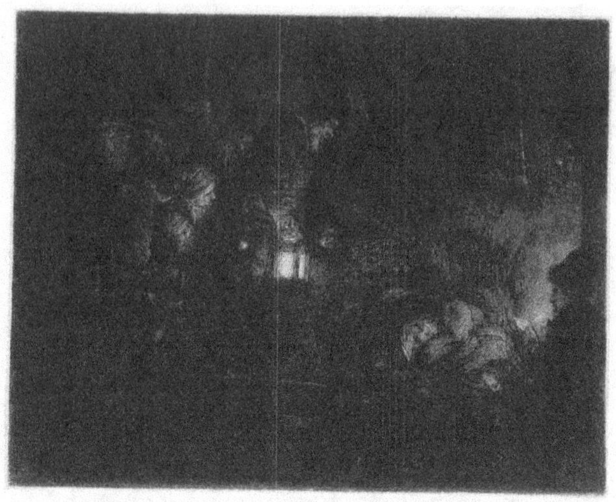

Rembrandt, The Adoration of the Shepherds, circa 1652, etching, drypoint and burin, 148 x 198 mm, B. 46.

Night scenes are the greatest challenge for any printmaker, because he has to fill the image with thousands of lines.

In the first half of the 1650s, Rembrandt produced several night scenes, one of which is the Adoration of the Shepherds from circa 1652. It is an endearing representation of the young mother looking lovingly at her baby, who is sleeping peacefully.

This was a sight that Rembrandt might have been familiar with from his home in Jodenbreestraat. Joseph is shown looking up from the book he is reading, surprised by the entry of the shepherds. Rembrandt included not only the shepherds in this scene, as tradition dictated, but also women and children. One of the shepherds carries a lamp, and takes off his hat as a mark of respect.

It is only with difficulty that we can see what happens in the darkness of the barn. Here and there, a ray of light shines on a face, making it just visible. In the first states of the print, a donkey and an ox can still be distinguished on the left side. The central figures - Mary and the Christ Child – are drawn with just a few lines, with the paper being left largely blank: it seems that this little scene radiates light.

However, Rembrandt was obviously not completely satisfied. How dark could a night scene be rendered without the representational element being lost? Eight proofs (states) were necessary for Rembrandt to obtain the desired result. In the first states, the right hand side of the image was rather light. Behind the Virgin, sheaves of grain can be seen.

In later stages, this part of the composition has been darkened, due to the artist filling the area with countless lines and hatchings. To obtain the warm velvety blackness, Rembrandt did not only use the etching needle, but reinforced part of the composition with a burin and drypoint. Come the fifth state, Rembrandt was apparently content, as he printed a small run of impressions. The burr of the drypoint lines wore away quickly during this print run, reducing the intensity of the black.

Rembrandt continued to work on the plate after the fifth state, changing the design in a number of ways. The eighth state is almost black, showing only the head of the Virgin, Christ and, in profile, the face of Joseph. The thin ray of light that connects the three main characters is an exceedingly clever compositional solution.

The tender intimacy between mother and child and the respectful, peaceful gestures of the shepherds make this image one of the most beautiful and memorable Christmas scenes ever created.

FAMOUS PREDECESSORS AS SOURCES OF INSPIRATION

Rembrandt, as mentioned above, had a huge collection of prints and drawings, which constituted an important source of inspiration. Rembrandt greatly admired Lucas van Leyden (1494-1533), and must have owned most of the engravings by this famous predecessor. It is well documented that the artist spent huge sums of money at auctions, sometimes paying between 200 and 250 guilders, a fortune at the time. Entire compositions and many details in Rembrandt's work can be traced back to Lucas van Leyden.

A good example of the artistic dialogue between Rembrandt and Lucas van Leyden is Christ Presented to the People, 1655, where the theme and composition are borrowed from the latter's 1510 engraving of the same subject.

Christ stands on an elevated stone terrace, flanked by Pontius Pilate's soldiers. Below the main event, the artist has depicted a small crowd of onlookers pointing to Christ, and in the background, the tower of a monumental building can be seen. From behind the balustrade of a palatial building, a group of wealthy people on a dais observes the events.

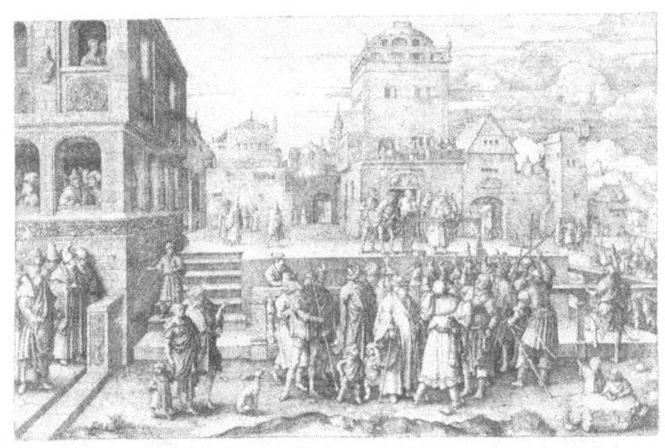

Lucas van Leyden, Ecce Homo, engraving, 1510.

Rembrandt based the subject and its main characteristics on the print by Lucas van Leyden. However, he zooms in on the main event, Christ as the prisoner of Pontius Pilate, bringing it to the foreground. The main scene is no longer drawn from a bird's eye perspective. Instead, Rembrandt chose a somewhat lower vantage point than the raised balcony on which Christ is standing. Thus, it feels as if we - the beholders - are part of the crowd of onlookers.

The event takes place in the courtyard of the monumental palace of Pontius Pilate, the Roman prefect of Judea. The viewer becomes a participant in the unfolding human drama: Pilate presenting Christ and Barabbas to the crowds in Jerusalem: "Ecce Homo" (Behold the Man). We can see Pilate asking the people whom he should set free - the murderer Barabbas or Christ. This act of grace was a tradition at the Jewish Passover. It is possible that Rembrandt found inspiration for his print in the new and imposing town hall of Amsterdam.

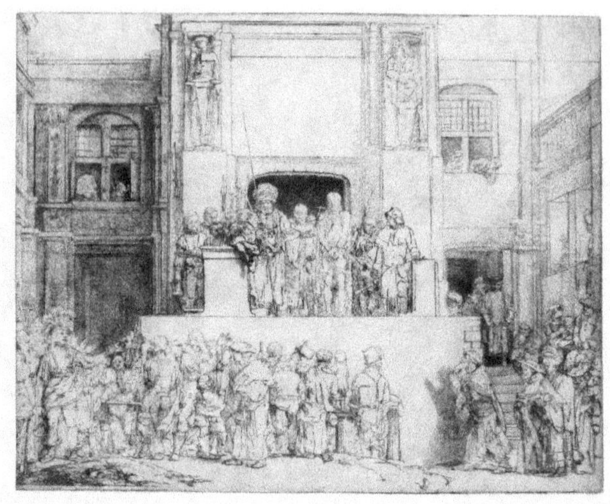

Rembrandt, Christ Presented to the People, 1655, drypoint, 358 x 455 mm, B 76.

In Amsterdam, like most towns in The Netherlands, justice was administered in this building. In the case of a death sentence, the convicted was often executed on scaffolding erected in front of the town hall.

The edifice in Rembrandt's print is reminiscent of the Amsterdam structure. Such buildings were decorated with statues of the personifications of Justice (a blindfolded woman, holding a balance in her hands) and Fortitude (personified by a male figure, like Hercules wearing his lion hide and holding a bludgeon).

Strength and impartiality, personified by these two figures, formed the basis for a fair and honest judicial system. In the niches above the terrace, Rembrandt has depicted life-size statues of Justice and Fortitude.

Rembrandt scratched the image with a drypoint-needle, which can be seen in the straight lines of the raised balcony on which Christ is standing, and the building around it. If one looks carefully through a magnifying glass, one can discern how the burr left along the grooves by the drypoint-needle points in one direction. Rembrandt drew these lines in the copper from right to left, like most right-handed people would do. On the paper, the burr is thus angled to the left. This is logical, as the print is the mirror image of the original plate.

If one looks attentively at the group in front of the dais, one can see how there is not one superfluous line in the design. Rembrandt has scratched the figures accurately and with tremendous precision. With astonishing mastery, Rembrandt drew the group of men and women directly onto the plate, without the aid of a finished and detailed study on paper, despite the considerable force required. There was no room for mistakes, and Rembrandt did not make any.

As with other etchings, Rembrandt composed the image with utmost care. Every detail, from the soldier with the feathers in his beret (left) to the people on the stairs, leads the eye of the beholder to the main scene: Christ and Pilate.

Images with a myriad of details, which require individual attention from the beholder, can often seem cluttered and unbalanced. The secret of Rembrandt is that his compositions never do, nor do the scenes appear artificial and contrived. This is true not only for this image, but, as we will see, for each and every print by Rembrandt.

While working on this composition, Rembrandt frequently printed the plate to see how work was progressing, and what it would look like on paper. The most beautiful impressions are made on Japanese paper.

The velvety, deep, black lines of drypoint are then seen at their best. Unfortunately, a drypoint etching wears quickly. After some twenty to thirty prints have been taken from the plate, the lines become greyish and the typical black fuzziness of the drypoint line disappears as the burr along the grooves is worn away. This happened to this print, and the image was not even finished! One has only to look at the blank spaces of the building to realise that the image needed more work.

Eight versions (states) of this print exist. In the fourth state, Rembrandt cut off a bit of the top edge of the plate. About thirty prints by Rembrandt of the fifth state are still in existence; most of these were printed on Japanese and Chinese paper. Even this small edition has caused considerable wear to the burr. This forced Rembrandt to rework the entire plate. At the same time, he changed the image significantly. The group of figures in front of the balcony, calling for the death of Christ, was burnished away completely by the artist.

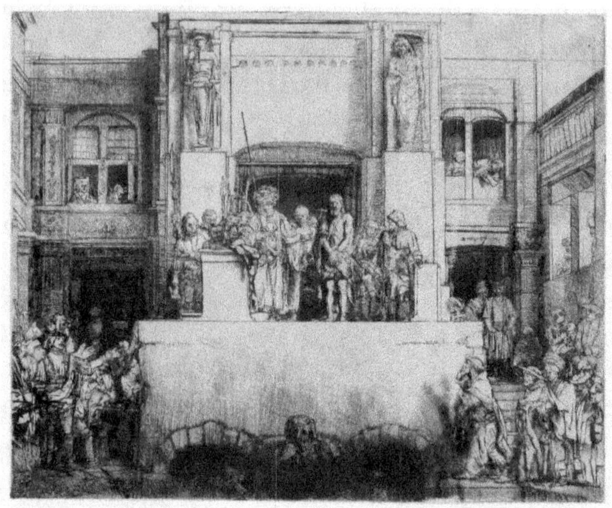

Rembrandt, Christ Presented to the People, 1655, drypoint, state VIII, 358 x 455 mm, B. 76.

By removing this group, the main scene is further emphasised. Nothing distracts from the dais on which Christ, Barabbas and Pilate are standing. In the intermediary stages, Rembrandt added two tunnel-like openings at the bottom with a statue of a river god in the middle. This statue was eventually removed. The eighth version is the final state of this print, even though the seventh state was signed by the artist.

PORTRAYING EMOTION. SELF-PORTRAITS AND BIBLICAL THEMES

The Bible was an inexhaustible source of inspiration for Rembrandt, and the stories gave him ample opportunity to portray emotion. But how does one learn to portray anger, surprise, sadness or despair? Time and time again, Rembrandt sat down before a mirror, and used his own face to study expressions. These images are intended as portraits of emotions, not as self-portraits. One of these minuscule prints is the famous and much loved etching in which Rembrandt has depicted himself with pursed lips. This little print is now known as Self-Portrait with Surprised Look.

If one looks closely at the prints and drawings by Rembrandt of biblical subjects, one is always struck by the enormous imaginative powers of the artist. One can see him trying to convey the emotional significance of a scene, always concentrating on the main protagonists. Though his scenes from the Old and New Testament may seem unrealistic, sometimes almost gothic fantasies to us in the twenty-first century, Rembrandt did his best to conjure up a world he believed to be true: the orientalist Levant.

Undoubtedly, Rembrandt was familiar with the robes and turbans of traders from the Middle East. He could have seen them in Amsterdam, the capital of the mercantile world in Rembrandt's days.

In his stately house, Rembrandt assembled a large collection of old, exotic clothes and fabrics, which were used as props in his works. One can see these objects in the many self-portraits he painted wearing oriental robes, or in the small prints in which he dressed up as an exotic king in furs, with a sabre resting against his shoulder.

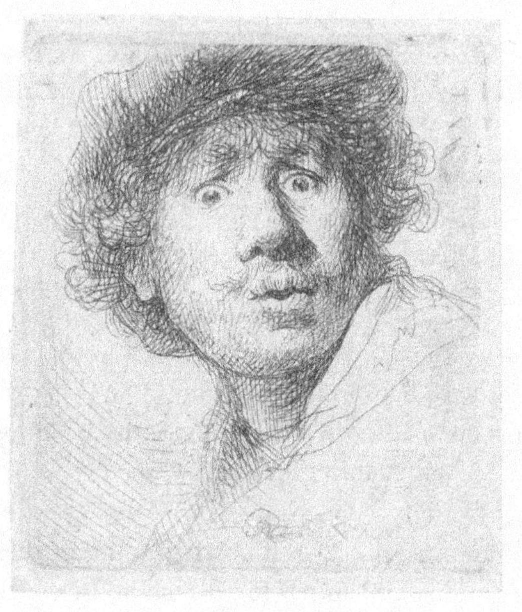

Rembrandt, Self-Portrait with Surprised Look, 1630, etching, only state, 51 x 46 mm, B 320.

A good example of Rembrandt's ability to envision the emotions involved in a dramatic biblical story is Abraham Casting Out Hagar and Ishmael, a scene based on the Old Testament.

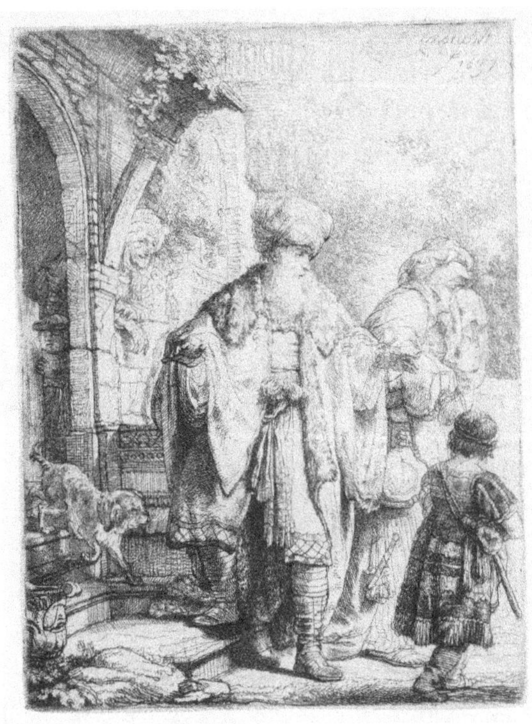

Rembrandt, Abraham Casting Out Hagar and Ishmael,1637,
etching and drypoint, only state, 125 x 95 mm, B 30.

The marriage of Abraham and Sarah had remained childless. Because of this unfortunate situation, Sara had given Abraham her slave Hagar, and Ishmael was born out of the union. Eleven years later, Sarah, by now an old woman, fell pregnant. After giving birth to Isaac, she forced Abraham to cast out Hagar and her son Ishmael. After some consideration Abraham consented, and sent Hagar and her son into the desert. This was the vivid moment that Rembrandt chose to depict - the episode was much loved by the artist and his pupils.

All dramatic elements of the story are included in the image: the despair and impotence of Abraham, the vile smirk of Sara in the window and the intense grief of Hagar, who realises that she and Ishmael will die of thirst or starvation in the desert. Neither Hagar nor Abraham knew that God would eventually save them. In the forceful imagining of this human tragedy, Rembrandt shows his unsurpassed mastery of pictorial storytelling.

TRACES OF DAILY LIFE

In some works, we can see traces of the daily life of the artist and his family. One immediately thinks of the magnificent double portrait of Rembrandt and Saskia, his wife, an etching made in 1636.

Initially, Rembrandt lived and worked in the house of the art dealer Hendrick Uylenburgh on the corner of Jodenbreestraat and Zwanenburgwal. It was probably through the art dealer that Rembrandt became acquainted with Saskia Uylenburgh, the cousin of Hendrick and the daughter of the well-to-do mayor of the city of Leeuwarden. They married in 1634.

Between 1636 and 1641 four children were born, the first three (Rombartus, Cornelia and then another Cornelia) died shortly after their birth, like many children in the seventeenth century. Only Titus, born in 1641, reached adulthood. A year after Titus was born, Saskia died after a long illness. Her death must have shocked Rembrandt.

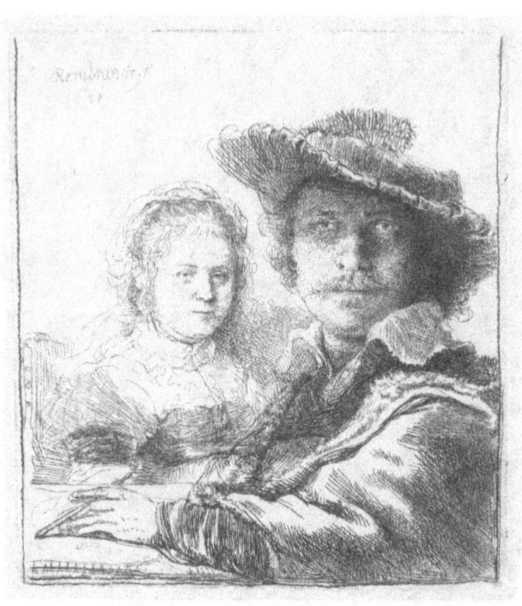

Rembrandt, Self-Portrait with Saskia, 1636, etching, 104 x 95 mm, B. 19.

One only has to look at the numerous portraits and paintings in which he used Saskia as a model to realise his love for his young wife. Two years after their marriage (1636), Rembrandt made a wonderful double portrait. Saskia sits at the table next to her husband, while he looks confidently into the mirror and portrays himself as a successful artist.

An image from 1641 or 1642 consists of several figural studies: a couple of beggars are included in the image, but also two sketches of a woman lying in bed, most likely Saskia, who never completely recovered after giving birth to Titus in 1641. Knowing that she would die shortly after the sketch was made adds poignancy to this intimate scene.

Rembrandt, Sheet of Studies with a Woman Lying Ill in Bed, a Beggar Couple, and Several Old Men, circa 1640-41, etching, only state, 151 x 136 mm, B. 369.

These kinds of sketches on copper are unique in printmaking. Six prints by Rembrandt with different studies in one image are known. A print was normally only printed after the artist completed the design, or - as we have seen - to check the progress while working.

These etched studies often show scenes sketched on the plate at different orientations: an old man, a shabbily dressed old woman beggar and a self-portrait. On three of the plates, Rembrandt sketched several portraits of Saskia. One explanation for the existence of these prints might be that the plates were initially meant to be cut up into smaller pieces.

Why Rembrandt printed the plates with the studies in fair numbers remains a mystery. Was it to satisfy the demand of collectors and their predilection for odd and rare states?

FAMILY LIFE AND THE THEORY OF ART

Seventeenth-century family life is also reflected in the image of two male nude models. In the background, very lightly etched, one can see a toddler in a walking frame. A woman attempts to make him come towards her. Endearingly, the child stretches his arms in the direction of the woman - a scene that could have been reflective of Titus' time as a toddler in the house of Rembrandt.

Around 1646, Rembrandt produced five etchings with nude models. These images were made in Rembrandt's studio. While the artist most likely sketched directly onto the etching plate, his pupils worked on paper. We know this for certain, since drawings by Rembrandt's pupils showing the same model in the same posture, but drawn from a slightly different angle, exist.

It is clear that the pupils must have sat in a circle around the model while drawing. Though the charming scene of the woman and toddler may have been fetched from daily life, it was included in this image as a lesson: just as a child has to learn to walk, an artist has to work hard to become a master. Diligence and discipline are required to learn a craft.

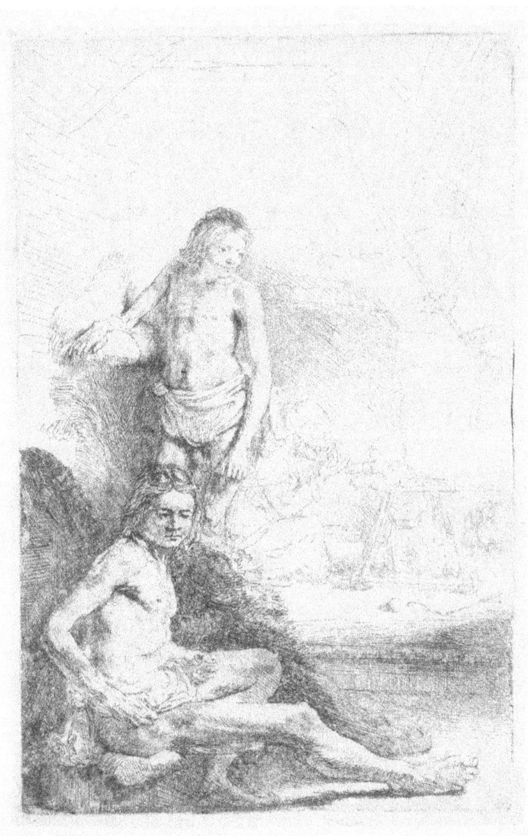

Rembrandt, Male Nude Seated and Standing (The Walking Frame), circa 1646, etching, 194 x 128 mm, B. 194.

Being able to draw a person convincingly and having knowledge of anatomy were prerequisites for any artist who wanted to train as a history painter, an artist specialised in painting images based on the Bible, history or classical mythology.

The print shows a glimpse of a seventeenth-century artist's workshop, and the prevailing attitudes to a painter's training.

Just like a child has to learn to walk, an artist had to be taught his craft step by step. The first step for any artist was to learn to draw the human body. Only when an artist had mastered proportions and anatomy could he paint figures in a natural and convincing way, with

49

the necessary gestures to express the emotions of the figures in a scene.

Practice was the only way for a pupil to gain the skills of the craft. Like a top that only spins when it is being whipped, the pupil has to work continuously and with great diligence. For this reason, Rembrandt chose to include the top and little whip in the scene: the child is still much too young for this kind of toy.

THE NETHERLANDS OF THE SEVENTEENTH CENTURY

Just as Rembrandt sometimes allowed the viewer of his prints a glimpse into his home, daily life in seventeenth century Amsterdam seeped into his etchings of beggars in ragged clothes, motley crews of vagabonds, itinerant street musicians and poor peddlers.

Rembrandt primarily based this kind of images, nowadays known as genre scenes, on artistic tradition rather than observation. As early as the fifteenth century, the fringes of society were drawn, painted or put into print. Especially loved as subjects were the festivities at fairs and yearly markets. The scenes included peasants brawling, drinking, flirting and kissing, dancing, fighting, vomiting and pissing. In short: all the unbound and unrestrained behaviour tolerated during carnivals, and even then only from the lower strata of society.

These extremely popular works often also included a throng of charlatans, petty thieves, pedlars and beggars. Quite often the images had a moral message: if one is to be granted eternal life, one has to abstain from the sinful, gluttonous, intemperate and lustful behaviour shown. Rembrandt engaged with this rich pictorial tradition, but gave it a unique twist.

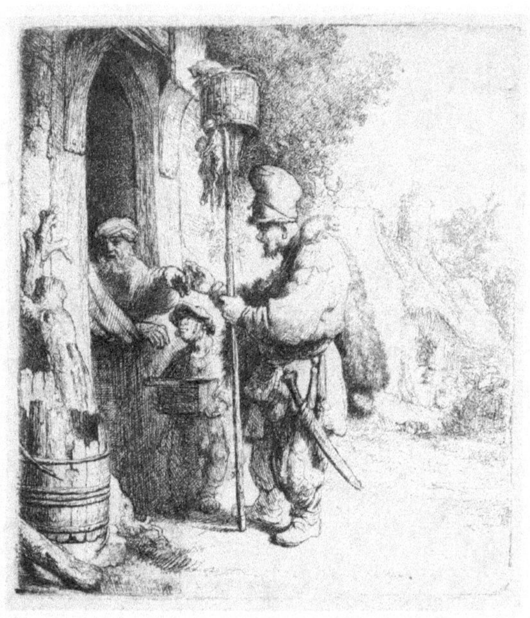

Rembrandt, The Rat-Poison Pedlar, 1631, etching, 140 x 125 mm,
B. 121.

The Rat Poison Pedlar is a clear example of a traditional subject in a seemingly realistic guise. At first glance, the image shows a Dutch hamlet with run-down farmhouses. A pedlar is trying to sell rat poison. Dead rats are hanging by their tails from the wooden cage on the pole, as proof of the effectiveness of the poison. A living rat sits on the shoulder of the pedlar, and more rats can by glimpsed in the cage. However, a number of odd details alert us to the fact that this scene may not be as realistic as we first thought. The old man leaning against the open door is wearing a turban, not exactly the kind of dress one would expect to find in a peasant village in The Netherlands. He rejects the pedlar and his little bag of rat poison and turns away in disgust.

The clothes of the pedlar and his little helper are noticeably eccentric, even if one is not a specialist in seventeenth century fashion. One look at Rembrandt's many portraits makes it clear that the clothes are at odds with Dutch dress of the period. The poison seller is wearing an exotic high hat, a sabre and a fur coat, unusual accoutrements for a poor salesman. A seventeenth century beholder must have immediately recognised that these clothes were outdated and bizarre.

Perhaps the image depicts an unknown story from the Bible. Whatever the subject of the scene, it is difficult to find a facial expression as striking as that of the wide-eyed, desperate and pleading look of the boy next to the poison seller. Discovering Rembrandt's secrets, like this unforgettable face, requires our time and patience.

This scene will probably send shivers down the beholder's spine: rats and fleas were one of the main causes of the recurring plagues, like the bubonic plague which repeatedly swept across The Netherlands in the seventeenth century, sometimes dragging a tenth or more of the population into their graves.

In Rembrandt's time, the cause of the disease was not yet known. However, the picture was very popular, and eleven artists made copies of the enigmatic scene. The print, made in 1632, is Rembrandt's first fully-fledged genre scene.

REALITY RENDERED?

The Rat-Poison Pedlar may owe more to convention than the reality of Dutch life in the seventeenth century, but with at least one scene we can be sure that Rembrandt relied on observing nature: a curled up, sleeping puppy. The tiny etching is based on a drawing he had made of a small dog on a leash, fast asleep in a makeshift doghouse. In the etching, he left out the doghouse, but one can still see the wooden floor on which the dog is resting.

By leaving the dog's head and its paw very light, Rembrandt managed to create form and depth in the composition. This dog, curled up in deep sleep, is the epitome of peace, and very memorable if you take the trouble of spending a few minutes looking at this tiny little picture of less than four by eight inches. It is arguably the sweetest dog in the history of art.

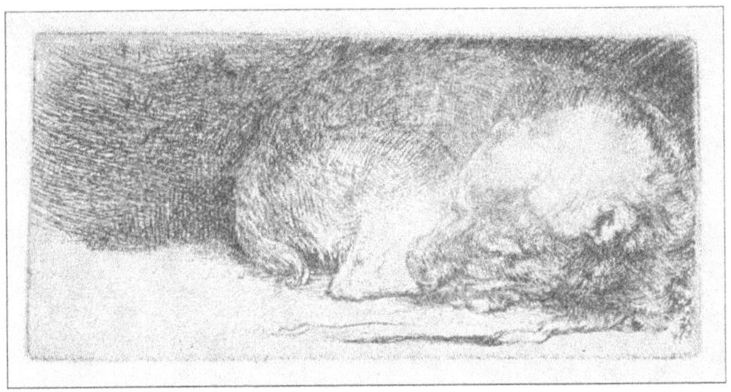

Rembrandt, Sleeping Puppy, circa 1640, etching and drypoint,
39 x 81 mm, B. 158.

In 1648, sixteen years after The Rat-Poison Pedlar, Rembrandt made an etching of a family at the door of a house receiving alms. In a drawing with the same subject, the man outside can be seen carrying a hurdy-gurdy, but in the etching only a small part of this instrument is visible. A blind hurdy-gurdy player was a popular subject in art as early as the sixteenth century. Like many times before, the choice of subject is traditional, but the way in which Rembrandt depicts the scene is novel. As a result, the image creates a convincing impression of being a realistic contemporary scene.

The first thing that strikes us is that Rembrandt has left almost half of the image blank. It therefore remains unclear whether the scene is set in a village or a city, though the facade of the stone building seems to suggest the latter. The atmosphere is that of a bright sunny day, but it is definitely not summer since the people are all wearing thick clothing.

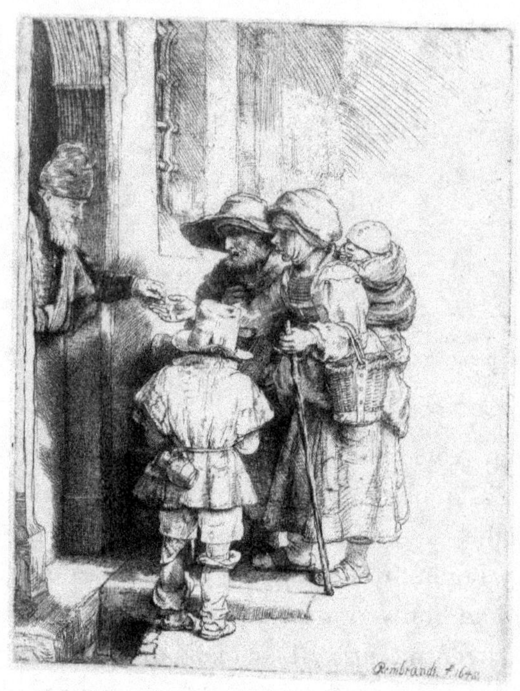

Rembrandt, Beggars Receiving Alms at the Door of a House,
1648, etching, drypoint and burin, 165 x 128 mm, B. 176.

Once again, we have to marvel at the subtle and imaginative way in which Rembrandt has crafted the composition. The back of the boy catches the light of the sun. His profile stands out against the woman and man, whose shape is shaded by the slanting light.

The shadows are delicately rendered by crosshatching. The gaze of the viewer is instantly drawn to the boy, and from there directed to the main action of the scene: the handing over of the coin.

The main focus of the image is the man putting his coin in the palm of the woman. The gesture is one of mercy and compassion. A number of details enliven the scene: the toddler on the back of the mother looking over her shoulder with squinting eyes, the pitcher hanging from the rope around the waist of the boy, the patched jacket, the skirt with the folded hem, and, above all, the woman's grateful countenance as she looks at her benefactor. This image embodies the concept of charity.

LANDSCAPES I: STROLLS AROUND AMSTERDAM

In 1639, Rembrandt moved to a monumental and expensive home in Jodenbreestraat. The city gate at the end of the street was little more than a stone's throw away. In just a few minutes, Rembrandt could be outside the city. Armed with a sketchbook he walked along the Kadijk, and from this dike he had an undisturbed view of the river Ij and the Zuiderzee behind it.

Through his numerous drawings and etchings, we can trace his walks around Amsterdam. We find him on the path on the banks of the river Amstel, and along St. Anthonisdijk and Diemerdijk. Occasionally, he walked west along the Spaarndammerdijk or Amstelveenseweg south of Amsterdam.

In the marshy polders around the city, Rembrandt made drawings of derelict, rackety farms. The open space of the landscape is highlighted by the low horizon. Much of the paper remained undisturbed and white.

The drawings have been called "studies of haziness" by an art critic, and they inspired Rembrandt to make landscape prints when back at home.

Some of the locations and cityscapes in the prints can still be identified, but Rembrandt was too much of an artist to be constrained by topographic accuracy - reality is enhanced by imaginary details. To the low polder landscape of the Amstel he added hills, or flourishes such as lovers in the shade of a willow.

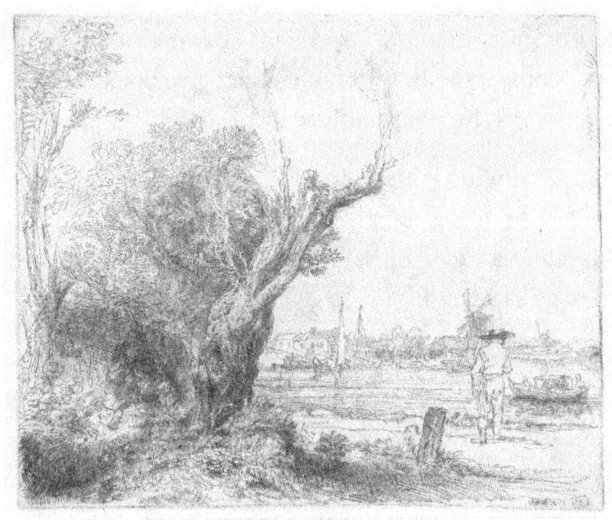

Rembrandt, The Omval, 1645, etching and drypoint, 184 x 225 mm, B. 209.

Rembrandt's first landscape prints appear around 1640. Five years later, in 1645, he made two etchings of landscapes along the river Amstel. One of them shows the Omval, just outside the city gates of Amsterdam, where the Amstel makes a sharp turn. Across the river, the houses and the windmills of the little village Watergraafsmeer can be seen.

A barge moves slowly over the almost still waters on this bright, sunny day. In the shade of an awning, several well-to-do citizens are sitting down. A man with a wide brim hat watches the barge go by. On the other side of the Amstel, the entrance to the canal around the Diemermeerpolder is visible.

As early as the eighteenth century, there was doubt about the location of the subject portrayed. In an inventory of 1679, the image is referred to as The Overtoom, a location slightly west of Amsterdam, where boats and barges had to be pulled across a low ditch. By the mid-eighteenth century, the print was described as The Omval in one of the first catalogues of Rembrandt's etchings. That name still stands.

The old, half-dead, willow in the foreground has caught the eye of many Rembrandt experts, and has been the focus of many discussions: could a willow have existed in this spot? It was most likely conceived in the imagination of the artist.

The reason is obvious and simple: a tree on a raised mound is unlikely in a dike along the river Amstel. Even stranger is the young couple depicted among the foliage. The boy places a wreath of flowers on the girl's head.

This fanciful element is important in the arrangement of the composition. The dark foreground creates, like the side wings of a stage set, a sense of depth. In addition, the small amorous scene in the foreground adds a bucolic atmosphere to this sunny landscape.

LANDSCAPES II: FANTASY AND REALITY

One of the most loved etchings derives its title from the main motif in the image: three trees. Rembrandt made this print, a combination of etching, burin and drypoint, in 1643. A thunderstorm is building up with clouds gathering above an extensive landscape. On the horizon, a city with a skyline resembling that of Amsterdam is just visible. Beside it, the surface of the Zuiderzee glitters in the last rays of sun. The three trees catch our attention, as the foliage stands out against the luminous sky.

This print became known as The Three Trees as early as the eighteenth century. The strong winds of a summer storm shake the trees, sweeping the branches to the left. The high vantage point gives depth to the image, leading the eye to the horizon. A sense of space is created by a subtle arrangement of bright, sunny patches, alternating with dark, shadowy strips.

The background shows the characteristic swampy meadows to the west of Amsterdam, whereas the foreground is reminiscent of the dunes near Haarlem, with its many pools and streams. As in The Omval, Rembrandt combines a realistic landscape with elements borrowed from his imagination or based on impressions from one of his walks in a fanciful but convincing way. Rarely is Dutch art of the

Golden Age completely true to nature. Rembrandt, like most seventeenth century landscape painters, manipulates reality to improve and enhance the mood of an image. It is art after all, not photographs.

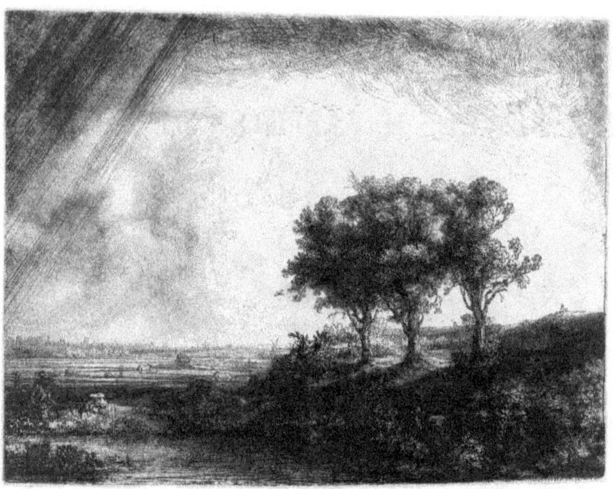

Rembrandt, The Three Trees, 1643, etching, drypoint and burin, only state, 213 x 279 mm, B. 212.

Little by little, we have become familiar with the way one has to approach Rembrandt's prints - to discover their secrets one must look extensively. Only by intense scrutiny does one notice the many narrative details contained even in this image. In the foreground, to the right, just above the surface of the water, an affectionate couple can be detected in the thickets.

A fisherman sitting on the grass with his wife is easier to spot. Less apparent are the shepherds in the meadows, with one huddled on a hill looking out over the landscape. On top of a dune, a draughtsman sits sketching, while further away a farm cart with a peasant moves slowly along.

The print is interesting from a technical point of view. The downpour is rendered with straight lines. These are grooves engraved into the plate with a burin, resulting in deep black lines.

The Three Trees is often described as Rembrandt's most impressive landscape print. During a poll to find out the most beautiful Rembrandt etchings organised by the Teylers Museum (2013) in Haarlem, The Netherlands, this print finished in third place, just behind a self-portrait and the famous Cornus Marmoreus, outshining any other landscape.

The print seems to have always been popular, as it was copied numerous times during the eighteenth and nineteenth centuries.

PORTRAITS OF FRIENDS

Rembrandt was one of the most important and prolific portrait painters of the Dutch Golden Age. Along with painted portraits, he made fifty etchings with portraits and character heads of mostly old men and women.

There is a noticeable difference between the painted and the etched portraits. While the paintings were created for the elite of Amsterdam, the etchings depict mainly people in some way acquainted with the artist; some of them were close friends of Rembrandt. In the portrait prints we see scholars, doctors, artists and ministers, belonging to a distinctly lower social class than the wealthy merchants and patricians in the painted portraits.

Portrait prints were often used as frontispieces in books, much like photographs of authors today. Sometimes comprehensive titles and eulogies were added to Rembrandt's etched portraits by other craftsmen. These prints functioned in a way similar to the modern business card and could be given to friends, relatives and acquaintances. It is probable that many of the portrait prints were made for this purpose, although the panegyrics are almost always missing.

One of Rembrandt's finest printed portraits is that of Cornelisz Claesz. Anslo from 1641, a wealthy cloth merchant and pastor of a Baptist church in Amsterdam. The congregation met for sermons in a building known as the large nail. A reference to this can be found in the large nail in the wall slightly to the right, above Anslo.

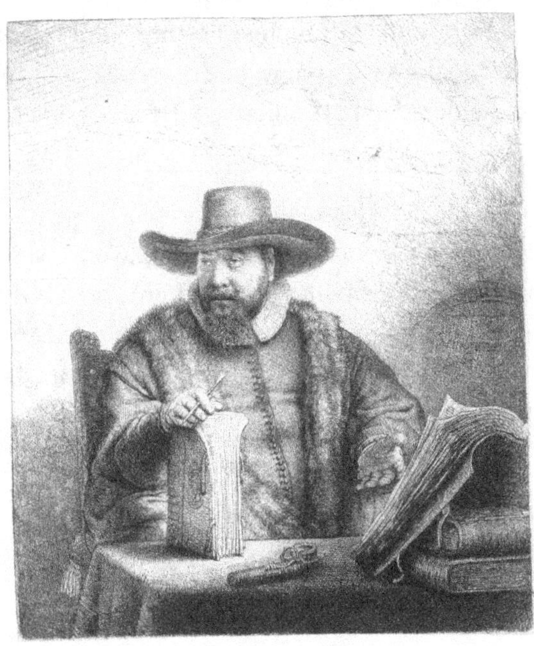

Rembrandt, Portrait of Cornelis Claesz. Anslo, 1641, etching and drypoint, 108 x 158 mm, B. 217.

For the portrait of Anslo, Rembrandt made a few studies and an elaborate, highly finished drawing in red chalk.

The lines of this drawing are slightly indented. The indentation of the outlines was caused by the pointed object with which Rembrandt traced the lines when copying the drawing onto the surface of the copperplate. The process involved a thin layer of black or red chalk dust being applied to the verso of the drawing.

Subsequently, the drawing was placed reverse down on the copperplate. By tracing the outlines with a pointed drawing utensil, like an etching-needle, the chalk on the back was pressed onto the copperplate. The method is similar to the use of carbon paper. It is logical that Rembrandt made an elaborate drawing for this work: a portrait should after all match reality as closely as possible.

Rembrandt only rarely made careful studies to be copied exactly onto the plate, a marked difference to the technique of most printmakers in Europe. Rembrandt's draughtsmanship and mastery of the etching-needle meant he was able to draw the scene in the etching ground without a detailed preliminary study alongside the plate.

However, a number of famous sketches have survived which correspond in some ways to scenes in prints. It seems that in these drawings, Rembrandt tried out and played with ideas for compositions and arrangements of figure groups. This sort of study exists, for example, for the previously discussed The Hundred Guilder Print, and for the family of the blind hurdy-gurdy player receiving alms at the door.

PORTRAITS OF THE ELITE: JAN SIX

Nowadays, Rembrandt's freer, more impressionistic, etchings are the most popular. In the seventeenth-century, however, collectors had a strong preference for finished and detailed prints. They had, in other words, a strong preference for prints looking like paintings in black and white.

One such print was the portrait of Jan Six (1618-1700), who was a member of an influential and wealthy Amsterdam patrician family. He commissioned several portraits from Rembrandt, and on another occasion he lent the artist money. In 1654 Six had his portrait painted by Rembrandt, resulting in a world-famous work that is still in the possession of the Six family. Seven years earlier, Rembrandt had made an etched portrait of Six reading by a window sill.

The image was obviously not intended to be an official portrait, since Six is dressed informally in an open-neck jerkin. This indicates that Jan Six and Rembrandt, who had known each other since 1641, may have been on close terms, perhaps even friends of a kind.

However, one should not forget that the men belonged to completely different classes of society, and that a friendship in modern terms was unthinkable. Even in this informal portrait, the artist highlights the elevated standing of the depicted. On a chair we see a bandoleer and a sword.

Rembrandt made three detailed studies in chalk for this portrait. He then transferred the contours of one of the studies onto the surface of the plate, using the process described above. The studies and the original plate are still in the possession of the Six family.

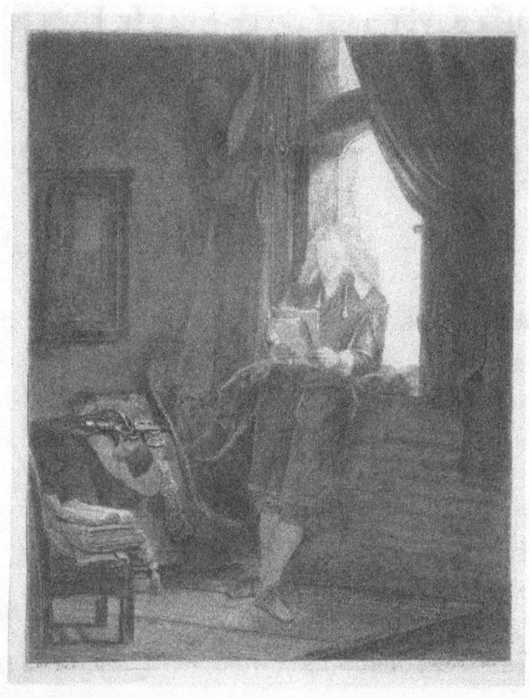

Rembrandt, Portrait of Jan Six, 1647, etching, drypoint and burin, 245 x 191 mm, B. 285.

The portrait of Jan Six is a highly finished and finely detailed print, like many portraits by Rembrandt or his contemporaries. These works are almost the opposite of his self-portraits and non-commissioned portraits. In those prints, Rembrandt seems only interested in the essence of a face, and large parts of the compositions are left untouched. To the modern eye, these light and free prints are far more attractive as they leave more to the imagination of the beholder.

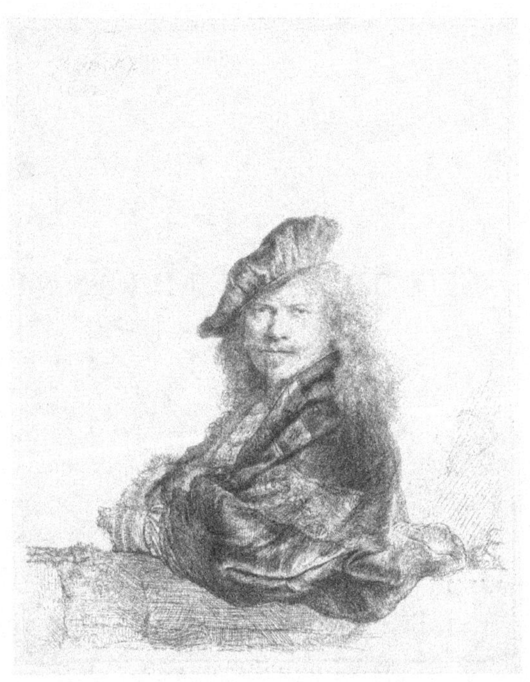

Rembrandt, Self-Portrait Leaning on a Stone Sill, 1639, etching and drypoint, 205 x 164 mm, B. 21.

SELF-PORTRAITS: REMBRANDT &
RAPHAEL

Rembrandt made an impressive array of self-portraits. The studies of his own face are called 'Tronies'. In these, he experimented with facial expressions, depicting emotions. Next to these 'selfies', as we would call them now, there are five self-portraits in which he presents himself as a self-assured and successful artist. The most memorable of these is a self-portrait in which he leans on a stone balustrade. The composition and manner, including the regal attire consisting of an expensive, fur-lined coat, are based on two Italian paintings found in the collection of the Amsterdam collector Alfonso Lopez (1572-1649).

It is clear that Rembrandt was familiar with both paintings, and he even made a sketch of one of them, the portrait of the Italian poet and playwright Lodovico Ariosto (1474-1533) painted by Titian (1487-1576) about 1510. The other painting is a portrait by Raphael (1483-1520) of Baldassare Castiglione (1478-1529), an Italian nobleman and the author of the book Il libro del Cortegiano, from circa 1515.

Could it be that Rembrandt competed with these two famous artists or tried to emulate them? Either way, with his self-portrait, Rembrandt showed that he was well aware of Renaissance painting. Besides these Italian pieces, Alfonso Lopez possessed one of the earliest painted works by Rembrandt, Balaam's Donkey, a scene based on the Old Testament, now in Paris (Musée Cognacq-Jay).

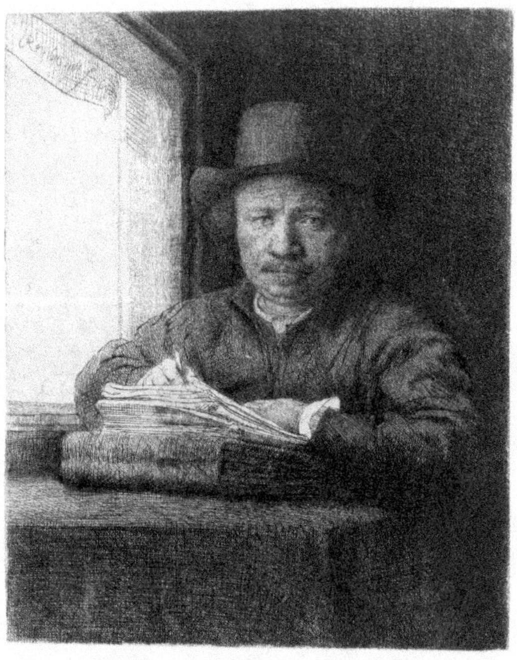

Rembrandt, Self-Portrait Drawing at a Window, 1648, etching, drypoint and burin, 160 x 130 mm, B. 22.

Almost ten years after the self-portrait discussed above, Rembrandt created a radically different image of himself. The artist looks the beholder straight in the eye, and on a table in front of him, a thick book provides him with a slightly sloping drawing surface.

By the way Rembrandt holds his drawing utensil, experts are certain that he is clutching an etching-needle. If this is true, he sketches the self-portrait directly in the etching ground on the plate. The earlier self-portrait was rough in comparison to this meticulously crafted image.

It has become an etched painting, where the background is completely shaded by hundreds and hundreds carefully drawn cross-hatchings. With all these lines, the artist tries to evoke tones and colour. To put it in another way, Rembrandt painted in black and white.

LOOKING BACK

In 1656 Rembrandt went bankrupt because of his enormous debts. Several causes led to this personal trauma. The taste and fashion changed at the end of the forties, resulting in fewer commissions for portraits. The first Anglo-Dutch War (1652-54) had major negative implications for Rembrandt's investments, and those of many of his contemporaries.

Most importantly, the artist was simply spending beyond his means, especially on his collection of art and objects. In 1656, a court drew up an inventory of his belongings, and a year later all his possessions were sold at auction.

The inventory is extremely interesting. Room by room, every object, piece of furniture or artwork is described. This document gives us the names of the rooms and their main function, resulting in a clear and intimate insight into an artist's home in the seventeenth century. No etching plates are mentioned, though they must have had substantial value. They may have been sold before Rembrandt's bankruptcy to the printer and publisher Clement de Jonge. In 1677, the year Clement de Jonge died, he had 74 plates by Rembrandt in his possession, a collection that remained complete until 1993.

The plates have been printed and reprinted by their various owners throughout the eighteenth and nineteenth centuries. This, of course, has caused considerable wear, and the plates have needed to be reworked and 'restored' time and time again.

The prints from the eighteenth and nineteenth centuries are regularly offered for sale at auctions. The auctioneers refer to these later prints as Watelet, Basan or Bernard-impressions: the names of the owners and printers of the plates in later centuries. It is possible to buy one of these prints for as little as a few hundred dollars. It goes without saying that a good early impression from the seventeenth century can be worth a fortune.

Rembrandt's etched landscapes, portraits, genre studies and biblical scenes never fail to appeal to our imagination, allowing us to daydream, or wonder at a lost world. This is the secret of Rembrandt's printed work. He asks us to look at his prints with undivided attention.

It takes time to enjoy and savour the many unexpected details in the prints, the compositional features, the facial expressions and gestures, and the huge variety of types and characters in his scenes. It is time well spent.

Suddenly, one realizes why Rembrandt is known as the greatest printmaker of the seventeenth century.

REMBRANDT - A BRIEF BIOGRAPHY

1609 – Born in Leiden

1620 – Enrolls at Leiden University

1624 – Apprenticeship with Pieter Lastman in Amsterdam

1626 – Workshop in Leiden and contact with Jan Lievens

1631 – Moves to Amsterdam

1631 – Lives and works in the house of the art dealer Hendrick van Uylenburg

1634 – Marries Saskia van Uylenburgh

1635 – Birth of Rombartus (dies after two weeks)

1638 – Birth of Cornelia (dies shortly after birth)

1639 – Purchase of a large house in the Jodenbreestraat

1640 – Birth of Cornelia (dies shortly after birth)

1641 – Birth of Titus

1642 – Death of Saskia after a long illness

1642 – Geertje Dircx works for Rembrandt and takes care of Titus

1647 – Hendrickje Stoffels starts work in the household

1650 – Geertje Dircx is locked away in an asylum in Gouda

1654 – Birth of Cornelia, daughter of Rembrandt and Hendrickje

1656 – Declared bankrupt

1657 – Rembrandt's belongings are sold at auction

1658 – The house on the Jodenbreestraat is auctioned

1660 – Titus and Hendrickje Stoffels become business partners, with Rembrandt serving as their employee and advisor

1663 – Hendrickje dies

1668 – Titus marries in February and dies in September

1669 – Titus' daughter Titia is born. Rembrandt dies on 4 October and is buried in the Westerkerk in Amsterdam on 8 October

FURTHER READING AND LINKS

Jonathan Bikker, *Rembrandt: Biography of a Rebel*, nai010 Publishers, 2019

curator Erik Hinterding, *Rembrandt: Etchings from the Frits Lugt Collection* (2 vols), Bussum / Paris 2008.

Christopher White, *Rembrandt as an Etcher. A Study of the Artist at Work*, New Haven / London 1999.

Gary Schwartz, *The Rembrandt Book*, New York 2006.

Eva Ornstein-van Sloten and Marijke Holtrop, *The Rembrandt House. A Catalogue of Rembrandt Etchings*, with additional material by Peter van der Coelen and Erik Hinterding, Zwolle /Amsterdam 2006.

http://www.rembrandtpainting.net

An overview of all of Rembrandts etchings can be found here:

http://en.wikipedia.org/wiki/List_of_etchings_by_Rembrandt

ABOUT THE AUTHOR

Michiel Kersten has worked for various museums in The Netherlands including the Print Room of the University of Leiden, Teylers Museum in Haarlem, Het Prinsenhof in Delft, the Frans Hals Museum and the Rembrandt House Museum in Amsterdam.

He specialises in the art of the Golden Age, particularly seventeenth century prints and drawings. Michiel has organised several exhibitions and contributed to a number of exhibition catalogues.

Rembrandt's etchings have always been a favourite topic, and he is particularly fascinated by the wealth of narrative content. With the realisation of the current publication, a long-cherished dream has come true - describing in plain language the greatness of Rembrandt's art, staying clear of art historical jargon.

Coming to the Netherlands and interested in the art of Rembrandt and his contemporaries?

Artetcetera, owned by Michiel Kersten, is specialized in gallery talks and guided tours in museums in Europe.

+ 31 (0) 6 1005 7228.
www.artetcetera.nl

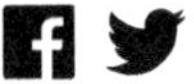

COLOPHON

Rembrandt Etchings - Looking at Rembrandt's Prints

Author: Michiel Kersten

Preface: Liesbeth Heenk

Paperback ISBN : 978-94-92371-30-0

Copyright: Amsterdam Publishers 2017-2019